INTERFACT ™

THE BOOK AND DISK THAT WORK TOGETHER

OCEANS

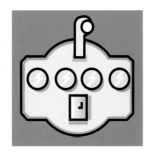

MINNETONKA, MINNESOTA

© 2001, 1997 Two-Can Publishing

Published by Two-Can Publishing
11571 K-Tel Drive
Minnetonka, MN 55343
1-888-255-9989
www.two-canpublishing.com

ISBN 1-58728-459-6

Photographic Credits: Front cover Ace Photo Agency
p.6-7 Ardea/Clemaagner p.8 Greenpeace/Morgan p.9 Ardea/Ron & Valerie Taylor p.12-13
ZEFA/Dr. D. James p.14 Planet Earth/Robert Arnold p.15 (top & bottom) Oxford Scientific Films/Peter Parks p.16 (top)
Ardea/J-M Labatt (bottom) Oxford Scientific Films/G.I. Bernard p.17 (top left) Planet Earth/Peter David (top right) Planet
Earth/Gillian Lythgoe (bottom) Planet Earth/Peter Scoones p.18 Ardea/Ron & Valerie Taylor p.19 Planet Earth/Peter David
p.20 Ardea/Clem Haagner p.21 (top) Planet Earth: Ardea/Jim Brandenberg (bottom) Ardea/François Gohier p.22-23 B. &
C. Alexander p.24 Ardea/Richard Vaughan p.25 ZEFA p.26-27 Ardea/François Gohier. Illustrations by Francis Mosley

3 4 5 6 09 08 07 06 05

Printed in China

INTERFACT ™

THE BOOK AND DISK ▽ THAT WORK TOGETHER

INTERFACT will have you hooked in minutes –
and that's a fact!

⬤ **The disk is full of interactive activities, puzzles, quizzes, and games that are fun to do and packed with interesting facts.**

Get some frank answers to all your questions about oceans from Frank Fish!

Click on Bubbles for a question

⬤ **Open the book and discover more fascinating information highlighted with lots of full-color illustrations and photographs.**

All shapes and sizes

A staggering variety of animals lives in the world's oceans. Their size, shape, and color vary enormously from creature to creature. To some extent, each marine animal's appearance depends on its life style and the ocean environment in which it lives. Sea anemones and sponges, for instance, stay rooted to the ocean floor for their entire lives and look more like plants than animals.

Fish are the most familiar marine creatures, but even their looks can be deceptive. Some species, such as eels, look more like snakes than fish. Others, such as the delicate seahorses, seem like animals in a class by themselves.

▲ Many sea animals are a silvery-blue color, but some have bright, bold markings. The most colorful animals live in clear tropical waters. Their striking appearance helps them to establish territory and frighten off enemies.

◄ The octopus is one of many curious sea animals. It has eight arms and a short, rounded body and lives on the ocean bed. To swim, octopuses squirt water from a special siphon in their body.

▲ About 5,000 species of marine sponges live on the sea floor. Some form fleshy sheets, while others resemble upright chimney stacks.

► The blue-spotted stingray is closely related to sharks. It glides above the seabed, feeding on slugs and worms.

► The waters near the bottom of the oceans are cold and dark. Many deepsea creatures have a light on their body that attracts prey. The deepsea anglerfish is very strange. If a male meets a female, he attaches himself to her. After a time, his body breaks down into a sperm bag, which then fertilizes the female's eggs.

DISK LINK
Design your own beautiful underwater world in Coral Creation.

What lives below the waves? Read up and find out.

◯ To get the most out of **INTERFACT**, use the book and disk together. Look for the special signs called Disk Links and Bookmarks. To find out more, turn to page 43.

23

BOOKMARK

DISK LINK
Remember how often tides rise and fall in order to survive Shark Attack!

Once you've launched **INTERFACT,** you'll never look back.

LOAD UP!
Go to **page 40** to find out how to load your disks and click into action.

What's on the disk

HELP SCREEN
Learn how to use the disk in no time at all.

These are the controls the Help Screen will tell you how to use:
- arrow keys
- reading boxes
- "hot" words

FRANK FISH
If you've got a question, Frank has the answer!

Get ready to go fishing for facts with Bubbles the seahorse! You'll get frank answers to all your questions about seas, oceans, tides, and waves from Frank Fish.

DEPTH GAUGE
Find out what goes on at different depths of the ocean!

Explore an interactive cross-section of the ocean. Learn about the different zones in the sea and the amazing animals that live in them.

CREATURE FEATURE
Visit a colorful undersea landscape and learn more about sea life.

Help a tiny fish find its way home by working out the identity of mystery sea creatures and answering true-or-false questions.

OCEAN EXPLORER

Investigate all of the world's major oceans, seas, gulfs, and bays.

Set off on a marine voyage of discovery aboard the fabulous Ocean Explorer! Find out all you need to know about the world's most important seas, oceans, gulfs, and bays.

SOMETHING FISHY IS GOING ON

Learn about the different parts of a fish's body.

When it comes to a fish's anatomy, do you know a pectoral fin from a pelvic fin? Try putting the correct labels on the interactive picture of a cod and find out!

CORAL CREATION

Get creative and conjure up a coral reef!

Assemble your very own coral reef on screen. Once your picture is finished, you can print it, color it, and keep it.

SHARK ATTACK

Get your teeth into the quiz or the sharks will get their teeth into you!

Put your knowledge to the test as you try to escape from the hungry sharks. All the answers are found in the book or on the disk.

What's in the book

*All words in the text that appear in **bold** can be found in the glossary*

Looking at the oceans

More than two-thirds of the world's surface is covered by vast oceans. They are the oldest and largest living **environments**, and life began there more than 3.5 billion years ago. But although oceans dominate the world map, we have only just begun to explore their hidden depths.

Without the fertile oceans, the earth would be dry and barren. Beneath them lie rugged mountains, active volcanoes, vast plateaus, and almost bottomless **trenches**. The deepest ocean trenches could easily swallow up the tallest mountains on land!

Seen from above, the world's oceans appear empty and unchanging, but beneath the surface hides a unique world where water takes the place of air. A fantastic mix of **algae** and animals live in these waters, from tiny **plankton** to the giant blue whale.

DID YOU KNOW?

● Salt is not the only substance found in seawater. Tiny traces of gold, silver, uranium, and other valuable **minerals** are also dissolved in the sea.

● Sound travels through water five times faster than through air. Dolphins navigate through the oceans by bouncing sounds off their surroundings and listening to their **echo**.

● Humans reached the deepest spot in the ocean for the first time in 1960.

DISK LINK
Dive into the ocean and explore the amazing world under the waves in Depth Gauge.

▶ Animals can travel freely through the water. Most sea animals breathe underwater, but some, such as dolphins and whales, need to come to the surface for air.

◀ In the tropics, the oceans are warm and clear. But around the North and South **poles** it is very cold, and parts of the ocean are always frozen. Huge chunks of ice, called icebergs, float here.

Dividing the seas

Strictly speaking, there is really only one ocean. It stretches from the North Pole to the South Pole and encircles the globe. However, because **continents** divide the water, people recognize four separate oceans – the Pacific, the Atlantic, the Indian, and the Arctic. Within these oceans are smaller bodies of water called seas, **bays,** and **gulfs,** which are cut off from the open oceans by land formations.

The Pacific is the largest and deepest of the four great oceans. It is larger than all of the continents put together. The word *pacific* means peaceful, but the water can be very rough. Waves more than 100 feet (30 m) tall have been recorded in the Pacific Ocean.

The Atlantic is the second biggest ocean, covering one-fifth of the world's surface. It is also the most important ocean for business – and therefore the busiest. Boats carrying cargo between the Americas, Africa, and Europe regularly cross the Atlantic.

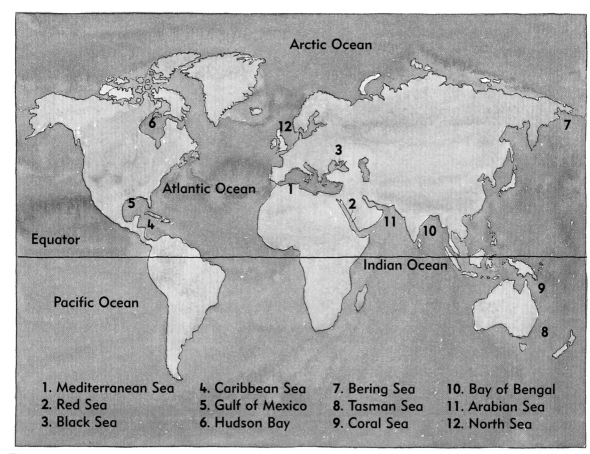

1. Mediterranean Sea
2. Red Sea
3. Black Sea
4. Caribbean Sea
5. Gulf of Mexico
6. Hudson Bay
7. Bering Sea
8. Tasman Sea
9. Coral Sea
10. Bay of Bengal
11. Arabian Sea
12. North Sea

DID YOU KNOW?

● It would take about 5,000 years for one drop of seawater to travel through all the world's oceans.

● The Atlantic Ocean is growing and the Pacific is shrinking. The continents move about 4 inches (10 cm) yearly, so the relative sizes of the oceans are always changing.

● Ancient Greek divers reached depths of 75 to 100 feet (22 to 30.5 m) in search of treasures. When a diver ran short of breath, he'd poke his head into a weighted diving bell filled with air.

DISK LINK
Investigate the oceans and all the major seas, gulfs, and bays in the Ocean Explorer.

▲ In warm tropical seas, where the water is shallow and clear, grow vast, rocky structures known as **coral reefs**. Reefs are made by small sea animals called **polyps**. Coral reefs hold a greater variety of life than any other part of the oceans.

Moving water

The world's oceans are always on the move. They travel in well-defined, circular patterns called **currents**. The currents flow like rivers, carrying warm water from the tropics and cold water from the poles. Where two currents meet, the colder water sinks, pushing warmer water up to the surface. In the Northern Hemisphere, currents travel in a clockwise direction. In the Southern Hemisphere, they travel counter-clockwise.

Oceans also change with the regular movement of **tides**. Twice a day, all over the world, oceans rise and fall along the coastlines. Tides are caused by the pull on the earth by the moon and the sun.

Tides and currents carry food and stir the water, mixing in oxygen, which sea animals need to breathe.

DISK LINK
If you want to learn more about what causes the tides, just ask Frank Fish.

OCEAN POWER

● Giant whirlpools, or maelstroms, can occur where two fast-rushing currents are forced through narrow channels.

● Earthquakes and volcanoes on the seabed can cause huge waves to crash on the shore. These giant waves are known as **tsunamis**.

Food for life

The basic food for life in the ocean is plantlike living things called **algae**. Two main types of algae live in the oceans.

The best-known ocean algae are the seaweeds found along coastlines. Limpets, periwinkles, and other shoreline creatures graze on seaweeds.

Seaweeds are not available to the animals of the open ocean. The most important **marine** algae are called phytoplankton. These tiny, floating algae grow wherever sunlight penetrates the water. Huge clouds of phytoplankton drift in the upper layers of the ocean, but they are too small to be seen with the naked eye.

Floating along with, and often feeding upon, the phytoplankton are tiny animals called zooplankton. The animals that make up zooplankton range in size from microscopic single-celled creatures to jellyfish and shrimplike shellfish called krill. This rich mixture of plankton is the foundation of all marine life.

PLANKTON FACTS

● Sailors crossing the ocean at night often see a soft glow on the water's surface. This is because some plankton produce flashes of blue-green light when they are disturbed.

● The very first life forms probably looked like today's phytoplankton.

● The largest animals in the world feed on plankton. Blue whales can weigh more than 100 tons (90 metric tons) and measure more than 100 feet (30 m) long. They strain krill from the water through a curtain of thin plates, called baleen, inside their mouths.

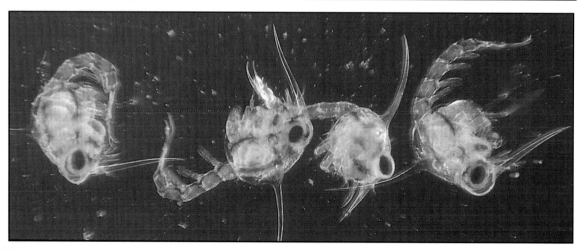

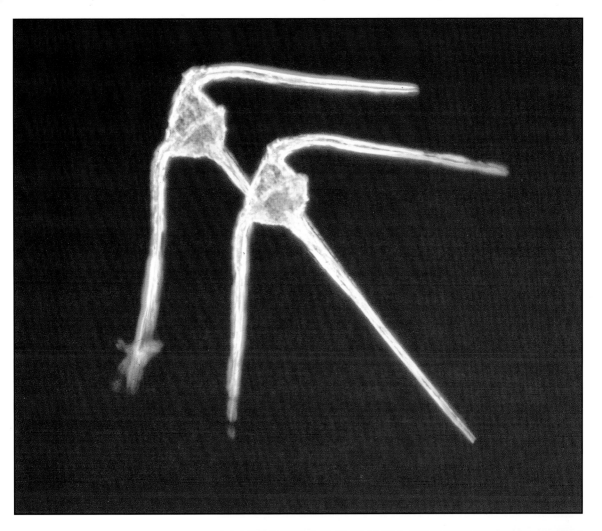

▲ ▶ Many of the tiny floating algae that form the phytoplankton join into chainlike strands. Others look like small ice picks, ribbons, or shells.

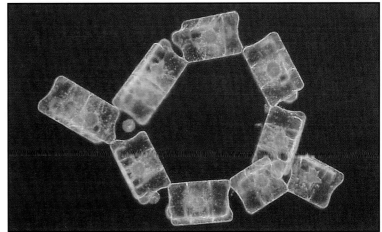

◀ Some zooplankton are single-celled life forms. Others are the larvae, or young forms, of fish or other sea animals.

All shapes and sizes

A staggering variety of animals lives in the world's oceans. Their size, shape, and color vary enormously from creature to creature. To some extent, each marine animal's appearance depends on its life style and the ocean **environment** in which it lives. Sea anemones and sponges, for instance, stay rooted to the ocean floor for their entire lives and look more like plants than animals.

Fish are the most familiar marine creatures, but even their looks can be deceptive. Some species, such as eels, look more like snakes than fish. Others, such as the delicate seahorses, seem like animals in a class by themselves.

▲ Many sea animals are a silvery-blue color, but some have bright, bold markings. The most colorful animals live in clear tropical waters. Their striking appearance helps them to establish territory and frighten off enemies.

◄ The octopus is one of many curious sea animals. It has eight arms and a short, rounded body and lives on the ocean bed. To swim, octopuses squirt water from a special siphon in their body.

▲ The waters near the bottom of the oceans are cold and dark. Many deepsea creatures have a light on their body that attracts prey. The deepsea anglerfish is very strange. If a male meets a female, he attaches himself to her. After a time, his body breaks down into a sperm bag, which then fertilizes the female's eggs.

▲ About 5,000 species of marine sponges live on the sea floor. Some form fleshy sheets, while others resemble upright chimney stacks.

▶ The blue-spotted stingray is closely related to sharks. It glides above the seabed, feeding on slugs and worms.

DISK LINK
Design your own beautiful underwater world in Coral Creation.

Hunters and the hunted

Many marine animals spend their entire lives filtering the water for plankton. However, they in turn are being hunted by other animals. It is estimated that for every 10 plankton-eaters, at least one hunter lurks nearby.

The shark is one of the most efficient marine hunters. Many shark species, such as great white sharks, mako sharks, and bull sharks, are perfectly designed killing machines. These sharks are streamlined for a fast life of hunting, and their mouths are lined with razor-sharp teeth. Sharks feed on fish, seals, turtles, small whales, other sharks, and even sea birds.

Although they have a reputation for eating humans, only about 50 of the 370 shark species are actually dangerous to people.

Not all marine hunters are as fearsome as sharks, but they can be just as dangerous. The pretty sea anemones look harmless, but they trap animals in their feathery tentacles, using them to inject poison into their victims' bodies. Jellyfish catch their prey in a similar way.

DEFENSE FACTS

● Octopuses, squids, and cuttlefish squirt ink to confuse their attackers, giving them time to get away.

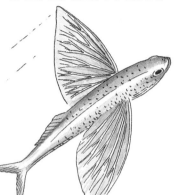

● Many soft-bodied sea animals, such as clams and snails, grow shells. Shells act as armor to protect the animal's body.

● Flying fish leap out of the water to escape their enemies.

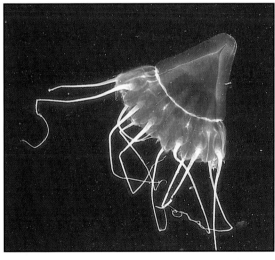

▲ Jellyfish, like sea anemones, catch prey in their trailing tentacles and poison them. Some of the most powerful poisons in the natural world are produced by jellyfish!

◄ Even when they are not chasing their next meal, most sharks must keep moving all the time or they begin to sink.

Taking to the water

During the history of life on earth, a small procession of land animals have returned to the oceans for their livelihood. Reptiles, mammals, and even birds have braved the deep, salty waters to take advantage of the rich bounty of sea life.

Whales, seals, turtles, and penguins are some of the animals that have left dry land to colonize the oceans. Although they may spend all or most of their time in the sea, they cannot breathe under water like true sea animals, so they regularly visit the water's surface for air.

Whales are the most successful ocean colonizers. People sometimes mistake them for fish. Whales spend their entire lives in the water, but most animals that have taken to the water must come back on land to **reproduce**.

DISK LINK
Test your knowledge of some of the amazing creatures that live in the oceans in the Creature Feature.

▲ Sea birds usually live on coastlines or on remote islands. But penguins spend more time actually swimming in the cold waters than most sea birds.

▲ Polar bears are considered marine mammals because they spend most of their time on or in the Arctic Ocean. Expert swimmers, their wide, furry paws are webbed to help them swim more easily.

▶ Sea reptiles, such as turtles, live in the warmer seas. They lay their eggs on sandy beaches.

Ocean resources

Throughout history, people always have harvested the rich ocean waters. As the human population has increased, people have turned to the oceans more and more to increase their supply of food and raw materials. Today, about 91 million short tons (83 million metric tons) of fish are caught each year. Crabs and lobsters are also popular seafood.

Modern fishing methods are often so successful that they ruin fish communities and upset the balance of ocean life.

Because of overfishing, many seas that once teemed with fish are no longer able to support large fishing fleets. And some whales and seals have been hunted to **extinction** for their meat, oil, or fur.

The nets used by many fishing crews also can cause problems. Besides fish, these nets also trap and kill turtles, sea birds, dolphins, and other marine creatures. In 1993, most countries agreed to stop using the most harmful kind of nets in international waters.

DISK LINK
You can learn all about cod in
Something Fishy Is Going On.

About a fifth of the world's oil and gas is mined from the seabed. The oil and gas are pumped through wells mounted on rigs that float or stand on legs attached to the seabed. Other ocean products include minerals, algae, and seaweeds.

▼ This North Sea trawler is small compared to the supertrawlers, which can be more than 295 feet (90 m) long.

OCEAN PRODUCTS

● Fish oils are used to make glues, soaps, and margarines.

● A rare gem called a **pearl** is formed inside the shells of certain oysters.

● Big nodules of iron, copper, and **manganese** are lifted from the seabed using suction pumps or are raked into nets by dredging machines.

● In dry lands, seawater is sometimes treated to create a fresh water supply.

● Seaweed can be eaten like a vegetable and is also used to help make ice cream, toothpaste, paints, and other everyday products.

Making the sea sick

Although we rely on the world's oceans for food, we often use them as a place to dump our wastes. Waste is pumped and dumped into the water, and **pesticides** and other **pollutants** are washed into the ocean by rivers and streams.

The pollution of the world's oceans is harmful. Many sea animals are injured, strangled, or suffocated each year because of floating debris, called flotsam. The high level of **toxic** wastes in a few seas is poisoning some animals and driving others away.

Landlocked seas, such as the Mediterranean Sea, are among the most polluted waters.

▲ Oil spills threaten marine life. This sea bird will die unless the oil is cleaned from its feathers.

DISK LINK
Remember what you read in the book if you want to survive the Shark Attack!

POLLUTION PROBLEMS

● Sealed barrels of dangerous radioactive and chemical waste have been dumped in some oceans, but no one knows if the containers are safe in the watery conditions.

● In some places around the world, pollution of the oceans has made local seafood unfit to eat.

▼ Busy ports can become deserted. The oil, sewage, and litter spilled into the water have made this harbor unfit for sea life.

DOS H^NOS GUERRERO

CU 1568

CU 1398

Save the oceans

Countries around the world are beginning to realize the importance of the oceans. International laws have been passed to restrict the amount of waste put into the water, and some marine mammals are now protected.

Countries on the shores of the dirtiest seas have begun cleanup programs. But there is still a lot to be done.

In recent years, oil spills caused by leaking or damaged ships called tankers have led to enormous damage. When oil is spilled on the ocean, it spreads in a layer on the surface of the water. This oil blocks the sunlight, upsetting the growth of plankton and affecting all marine life. Oil that reaches the shore ruins beaches and kills seals, birds, and other animals.

Activities that once were considered to be harmless have now been found to have damaging effects on marine life. Cables laid on the ocean floor disturb some bottom-dwelling creatures and confuse many fish. Sharks bite into the cables, mistaking them for prey.

The noisy hustle and bustle from boats, busy coastal resorts, and ocean-based industries frightens seals, dolphins, and other animals from their traditional breeding grounds.

Whales – the giants of the natural world – have been hunted for their oil and meat for so long that many kinds are now endangered. As a result, they have become a strong international symbol of ocean conservation.

Most countries agree that people must stop killing whales, and laws have now been made to protect the largest whale species. But, sadly, some people eat whale meat as an expensive delicacy, and whale hunting continues in a few countries.

Dakuwaca fights for his life

This tale is told by the people of the island country of Fiji, who depend on the ocean for food and transportation.

Long ago, sharks were the rulers of the islands that make up Fiji, a country in the Pacific Ocean. Each island had its own particular shark that lived beside the reef entrance to the island. These sharks patrolled the waters of their territory, challenging anyone who dared to come near. They allowed friends in but fought with hostile sharks until they paid a tribute.

Dakuwaca thought himself the greatest of all the sharks. He was big and fierce and enjoyed nothing better than a fight with another shark. He had never lost a fight, and he was quite sure he never would. He cared nothing for the terrible storms that his fights caused, whipping up the waters so that the islanders were tossed about in their boats. Often massive waves from the ocean swept away island houses.

Dakuwaca was patrolling his reef one day when he came across a shark named Masilica. Masilica was the mischief-maker among the sharks. He did not fight much himself but, with his wily ways, he had caused more fights than most sharks had fought!

"Good day, Dakuwaca," he said. "I suppose you're off for another fight. It's amazing, the way you always beat the other sharks. I wish I were as good a fighter as you."

"No other shark is as good a fighter as I am," said Dakuwaca. "Hardly anyone bothers to challenge me any more. They all know that I am so much stronger than they. In fact, it's getting very dull around here."

"Perhaps if you really want a good fight, you should go over to Kandavu Island. I hear there's a creature well worth fighting there, a mighty monster that guards the reef. But no one ever goes there because they are much too afraid," said Masilica, with a sly glint in his eye. "Of course, I'm not suggesting that you're frightened. You're much too brave. And I'm sure none of the other sharks thinks that you're afraid either."

Dakuwaca thrashed his tail through the water. Of course he wasn't afraid; what a suggestion! But if the other sharks thought he was afraid, he had better do something at once. Almost before Masilica had finished speaking, Dakuwaca set off towards Kandavu, determined to challenge the fearsome monster.

As Dakuwaca approached Kandavu, he heard a deep, powerful voice calling from the shore. Dakuwaca had never heard anything like it before, and he found himself trembling with fright.

"How foolish," he told himself. "Nothing on the shore can harm me." And he swam on.

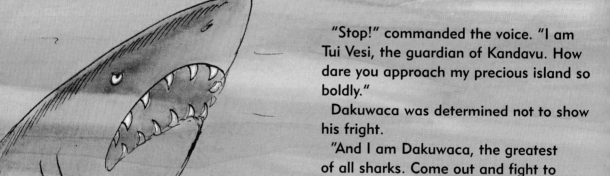

"Stop!" commanded the voice. "I am Tui Vesi, the guardian of Kandavu. How dare you approach my precious island so boldly."

Dakuwaca was determined not to show his fright.

"And I am Dakuwaca, the greatest of all sharks. Come out and fight to defend your island."

"I am a land guardian and so cannot come into the water to fight you," said Tui Vesi. "I shall send one of my servants to fight you instead. But be warned! It is a great and terrible monster, and it would be much better if you left now."

"No one is braver or stronger than I," said Dakuwaca. "I am not afraid of anything. I will fight your servant."

He swam around the mouth of the reef, watching and waiting for his opponent. His body was strong and quick, and his teeth were sharp.

Suddenly a giant arm appeared from the reef and grabbed him. A giant octopus! This wasn't what Dakuwaca was expecting at all!

Dakuwaca thrashed and twisted to rid himself of the arm. His sharp teeth were quite useless because he could not bend his body to bite at the arm. The arm loosened as he twisted and, for a moment, Dakuwaca thought he was free.

But no, two more arms whipped around so that Dakuwaca could no longer move at all. And the arms began to squeeze, tighter and tighter until he could bear it no longer.

"Have mercy," Dakuwaca gasped. "Forgive my terrible presumption, Tui Vesi."

The arms of the octopus loosened slightly, and Tui Vesi's mighty voice boomed out into the waters once more.

"I will release you, Dakuwaca, providing that you promise to guard the people of my island from sharks that might attack them when they go out in their canoes."

"Yes, yes! Of course I will," Dakuwaca agreed.

At once the octopus released Dakuwaca, and he sank to the seabed exhausted. When he had recovered, he set off back to his own territory. He kept his promise and protected the island of Kandavu from other sharks. In spite of his fears, the other sharks believed his claim that he had made friends with the mighty guardian of Kandavu and feared him just as much as before. All except Masilica, that is, who would occasionally drop the word *octopus* into conversation and dash away as Dakuwaca snapped at him.

And that is why, while other fishermen of the Fiji islands fear for their lives because of the sharks, the men of Kandavu ride happily in their canoes.

True or false?

Which of these facts are true and which are false?
If you have read this book carefully, you will know the answers!

1. Almost one-third of the world's surface is covered by oceans.

2. The paws of a polar bear are webbed.

3. Dolphins and whales can stay under water for several hours.

4. Sound travels through water five times faster than through air.

5. The world's four oceans are the Pacific, the Atlantic, the Aegean, and the Mediterranean.

6. It takes 5,000 years for one drop of seawater to travel through all the world's oceans.

7. Tsunamis are caused by underwater volcanic explosions and earthquakes.

8. Plankton is a rich mixture made up of the debris from seaweed.

9. Octopuses have 12 arms and feed mainly on seals.

10. Seaweed is used to help make ice cream.

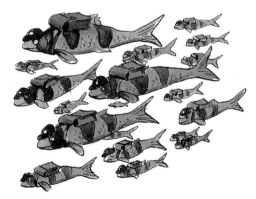

11. Fish travel in schools until they learn how to protect themselves.

12. Sharks must keep moving all the time or they will sink.

ANSWERS: 1.F 2.T 3.F 4.T 5.F 6.T 7.T 8.F 9.F 10.T 11.F 12.T

Glossary

Algae are plantlike living things that grow under water, such as seaweeds.

Bay is part of an ocean or other large body of water that forms a curve in the shoreline. It is bordered on the coastline by headlands or capes.

Continent is a large piece of land or mainland. It is larger than a normal island and usually divided into several countries (except for the continent of Australia).

Current is the movement of a body of water in a particular direction. Ocean currents may be very strong and extend over great distances.

Echo is the repetition of a noise caused by the bouncing back of sound waves from a solid object. Marine mammals such as dolphins use echoes to locate food and to avoid obstacles.

Environment is the set of conditions in the area where an animal lives. The animal's survival depends on how well it can respond to these conditions.

Coral reef is a colorful ridge formation, usually under water. It is made up of the hard outer casing produced by a colony of millions of tiny animals called polyps.

Extinction is when the last member of a species dies out. This may be due to overhunting by humans, the arrival of a rival animal or plant, or changes in the species' environment.

Gulf is a part of a sea or ocean that loops into the neighboring coastline. It is narrower at its mouth than a bay.

Landlocked means surrounded by land.

Manganese is a brittle, grayish-white metallic element, often used in making steel.

Marine means connected with the sea. Marine animals are those that live in the sea.

Minerals are chemical compounds found in rocks. Some of them are useful to humans and are mined.

Pearl is a small gem, usually round and white, cream, or bluish-gray. It slowly forms as a protective layer around a grain of sand or other object that irritates the soft flesh inside an oyster's shell.

Pesticides are chemicals used to kill pests that feed on crops. Some may be dangerous to other creatures, too.

Plankton is a rich mixture of many types of small sea life. A large variety of sea animals feed on it.

Poles are found at the exact north and south ends of the earth.

Pollutant is a dirty and poisonous product that damages the environment.

Polyp is a small animal that lives in colonies. The hard outer skeletons of polyps form coral.

Reproduction is when adult creatures produce new, young individuals.

Tide is the regular rising and falling of the sea. It is caused by the pull of the moon and the sun on the earth.

Toxic means poisonous.

Trench is a deep furrow. The Mariana Trench near Guam is the deepest known place in any ocean.

Tsunami is a huge sea wave caused by an underwater earthquake or volcanic eruption.

Lab pages

Photocopy these sheets and use them to make your own notes.

Lab pages

Loading your INTERFACT disk

INTERFACT is easy to load. But, before you begin, quickly run through the checklist on the opposite page to ensure that your computer is ready to run the program.

Your INTERFACT CD-ROM will run on both PCs with Windows and on Apple Macs. To make sure that your computer meets the system requirements, check the list below.

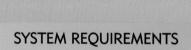

SYSTEM REQUIREMENTS

PC
- 486DX2/66 Mhz Processor
- Windows 3.1, 3.11, 95, 98 (or later)
- 8 Mb RAM (16 Mb recommended for Windows 95 and 24 Mb recommended for Windows 98)
- VGA colour monitor
- SoundBlaster-compatible soundcard

APPLE MACINTOSH
- 68020 processor
- system 7.0 (or later)
- 16 Mb of RAM

LOADING INSTRUCTIONS

You can run INTERFACT from the disk – you don't need to install it on your hard drive.

PC WITH WINDOWS 95 OR 98

The program should start automatically when you put the disk in the CD drive. If it does not, follow these instructions.

1. Put the disk in the CD drive
2. Open MY COMPUTER
3. Double-click on the CD drive icon
4. Double-click on the icon called OCEANS

PC WITH WINDOWS 3.1 OR 3.11

1. Put the disk in the CD drive
2. Select RUN from the FILE menu in the PROGRAM MANAGER
3. Type D:\OCEANS (Where D is the letter of your CD drive)
4. Press the RETURN key

APPLE MACINTOSH

1. Put the disk in the CD drive
2. Double click on the INTERFACT icon
3. Double click on the icon called OCEANS

CHECKLIST

● Firstly, make sure that your computer and monitor meet the system requirements as set out on page 40.

● Ensure that your computer, monitor and CD-ROM drive are all switched on and working normally.

● It is important that you do not have any other applications, such as wordprocessors, running. Before starting INTERFACT quit all other applications.

● Make sure that any screen savers have been switched off.

● If you are running INTERFACT on a PC with Windows 3.1 or 3.11, make sure that you type in the correct instructions when loading the disk, using a colon (:) not a semi-colon (;) and a back slash (\) not a forward slash (/). Also, do not use any other punctuation or put any spaces between letters.

How to use INTERFACT

INTERFACT is easy to use.
First find out how to load the program
(see page 40), then read these simple
instructions and dive in!

You will find that there are lots of different features to explore.
Choose the feature you want to play using the controls on the right-hand side of the screen. You will see that the main area of the screen changes as you click on different features.

For example, this is what your screen will look like when you play Something Fishy Is Going On, which is all about the parts of a fish's anatomy. Once you've selected a feature, click on the main screen to start playing.

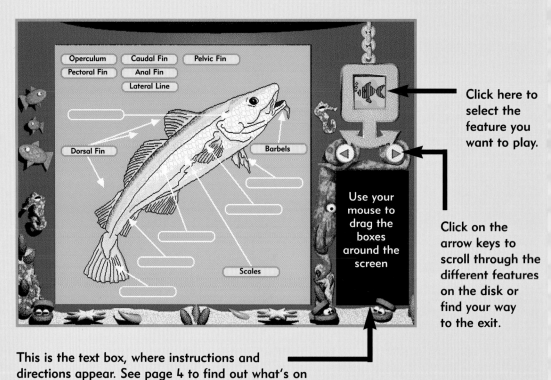

Operculum   Caudal Fin   Pelvic Fin
Pectoral Fin   Anal Fin
Lateral Line

Dorsal Fin

Barbels

Scales

Click here to select the feature you want to play.

Use your mouse to drag the boxes around the screen

Click on the arrow keys to scroll through the different features on the disk or find your way to the exit.

This is the text box, where instructions and directions appear. See page 4 to find out what's on the disk.

DISK LINKS

When you read the book, you'll come across Disk Links. These show you where to find activities on the disk that relate to the page you are reading. Use the arrow keys to find the icon on screen that matches the one in the Disk Link.

DISK LINK
Why are sharks' teeth always so sharp? Find out in Creature Feature.

BOOKMARKS

As you explore the features on the disk, you'll bump into Bookmarks. These show you where to look in the book for more information about the topic on screen. Just turn to the page of the book shown in the Bookmark.

23

LAB PAGES

On pages 36–39, you'll find grid pages to photocopy. These are for making notes and recording any thoughts or ideas you may have as you read the book.

HOT DISK TIPS

- After you have chosen the feature you want to play, remember to move the cursor from the icon to the main screen before clicking the mouse again.

- If you don't know how to use one of the on-screen controls, simply touch it with your cursor. An explanation will pop up in the text box!

- Keep a close eye on the cursor. When it changes from an arrow ➔ to a hand, click your mouse and something will happen.

- Any words that appear on screen in blue and underlined are "hot." This means you can touch them with the cursor for more information.

- Explore the screen! There are secret hot spots and hidden surprises to find.

Troubleshooting

If you have a problem with your INTERFACT disk, you should find the solution here. If you still have a problem, send us an email at helpline@two-canpublishing.com.

QUICK FIXES   Run through these general checkpoints before consulting COMMON PROBLEMS (see opposite page).

QUICK FIXES

PC WITH WINDOWS 3.1 OR 3.11

1 Check that you have the minimum system requirements: 386/33Mhz, VGA color monitor, 4Mb of RAM.

2 Make sure you have typed in the correct instructions: a colon (:) not a semi-colon (;) and a back slash (\) not a forward slash (/). Also, do not put any spaces between letters or punctuation.

3 It is important that you do not have any other programs running. Before you start **INTERFACT**, hold down the Control key and press Escape. If you find that other programs are open, click on them with the mouse, then click the End Task key.

QUICK FIXES

PC WITH WINDOWS 95

1 Make sure you have typed in the correct instructions: a colon (:) not a semi-colon (;) and a back slash(\) not a forward slash (/). Also, do not put any spaces between letters or punctuation.

2 It is important that you do not have any other programs running. Before you start **INTERFACT**, look at the task bar. If you find that other programs are open, click with the right mouse button and select Close from the pop-up menu.

MACINTOSH

1 Make sure that you have the minimum system requirements: 68020 processor, 640x480 color display, system 7.0 (or a later version), and 4Mb of RAM.

2 It is important that you do not have any other programs running. Before you start **INTERFACT**, click the application menu in the top right-hand corner. Select each of the open applications and select Quit from the File menu.

COMMON PROBLEMS

 Symptom: Cannot load disk.
Problem: There is not enough space available on your hard disk
Solution: Make more space available by deleting old applications and files you don't use until 6Mb of free space is available.

 Symptom: Disk will not run.
Problem: There is not enough memory available.
Solution: *Either* quit other open applications (see Quick Fixes) *or* increase your machine's RAM by adjusting the Virtual Memory.

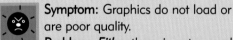 **Symptom:** Graphics do not load or are poor quality.
Problem: *Either* there is not enough memory available *or* you have the wrong display setting.
Solution: *Either* quit other applications (see Quick Fixes) *or* make sure that your monitor control is set to 640x480x256 or VGA.

 Symptom: There is no sound (PCs only).
Problem: Your sound card is not Soundblaster compatible.
Solution: Try to configure your sound settings to make them Soundblaster compatible (refer to your sound card manual for more details).

 Symptom: Your machine freezes.
Problem: There is not enough memory available.
Solution: *Either* quit other applications (see Quick Fixes) *or* increase your machine's RAM by adjusting the Virtual Memory.

 Symptom: Text does not fit neatly into boxes and "hot" copy does not bring up extra information.
Problem: Standard fonts on your computer have been moved or deleted.
Solution: Reinstall standard fonts. The PC version requires Arial; the Macintosh version requires Helvetica. See your computer manual for further information.

Index